...N ADD THEREST OT THE WATER + OLIVE OIL
...THIS IN THE FLOUR COMPOSITIO...
...TO A BOWL PUT ON THE SIDE COVERED WITH
...TOWL TO PROVDE IN A MIDSTATE WARM AREA.

...IN THE FLOUR COMPOSITION DOUBLES THE SIZ...
...KE OUT ON WORK SURFACE, CUT INTWO
...FORM TWO BALLS ROLL THEM OUT AND
...THEM INTO A OMELETTE PAN.
...WAYS BUTTER AND DUST WITH FLOUR TO
...OID SICKING OT THE BREAD).
...UNDER KITCHEN TOWL FOR 20 MINUTES.
...MORE TOWL AND PUNCH HOLES IN THE
...UGH WITH FINGERS. SPRINKEL OLIDE OIL
...R THE DOUGH AND SPREAD OUT WITH YOUR
...D WITHOUT PRESSING ON THE DOUGH.
...RINKEL SALT OVER THE DOUGH.
...IN OVEN 400°F FOR ABOUT 15 TO 20 MI...
...CREATE STEAM IN YOUR OVEN YOU CAN
...CK A 1/2 CUP OT WATER IN OVEN AND
...CKLY CLOSE THE OVEN.

...N FINISHED WITH BAKING PROCCEN TAKE
...AND PUT ON WIRE RACK. IN DIFFERENC...

CHARTING
CULINARY
COURSES

SIMPLE YET ELEGANT RECIPES FOR PEOPLE WHO LOVE TO COOK
FROM YACHT CHEF DIRK DE CUYPER

A.B. Hirschfeld Press
Denver, Colorado

© 2000 by Charles Gallagher
Food photography © 2000 by Joe Coca

Project development and design: Barbara Ciletti
Editor and content advisor: Judith Durant
Design and production: Keith Rosenhagen/Graphic Relations
Food and photo styling: Judith Durant and Barbara Ciletti
Selected commentary: Hsaio Ching Chou
Location photos: Gary Olsen

Library of Congress Card Number: 00-102036

Photos on page 10 ©Showboats International, reprinted with permission.

10 9 8 7 6 5 4 3 2 1

First Edition

Published by A.B. Hirschfeld Press
5200 Smith Road
Denver, Colorado 80216

Every effort has been made to ensure that the information in this book is
accurate. However, due to differing conditions, tools and individual skills,
the publisher cannot be responsible for any injuries, loses or other damages
that may result from the information in this book.

ISBN 0-9678752-0-X

Printed in the United States of America

Foreword

I began my yachting career in 1971 as a deckhand aboard a classic 112-foot Trumpy motor yacht that was built in 1931. In all my experiences at sea, one thing remains constant — passengers love to indulge in the finest culinary delights a chef can produce. While the beautifully exotic ports and everything that yachting has to offer provide wonderful memories, food is an extremely important part of the whole experience.

People say that food just tastes better after a hard day of water skiing, diving, beach combing, and sunbathing, but this is even more true when the food is prepared and presented by a professional like Dirk De Cuyper. Dirk believes that presentation is every bit as important as taste, and he combines his extensive culinary training with the best of the available foods wherever we are.

Here on Cakewalk, we are fortunate to have something that some other yachts lack — the Cakewalk's owners truly appreciate fine dining and enjoy being surprised by every new dish. We also enjoy a team spirit with the owners, crew, and chef, a spirit that makes it possible to produce the culinary extravaganzas you will find here.

– William C. Zinser
  Captain, Cakewalk

Contents

Recipes

Acknowledgments

Any chef worthy of culinary credibility knows that great food comes from quality ingredients, proven techniques and a certain touch of inspired creativity. So many times, these very elements converge to grace our tables, and later warm our thoughts with memories of good dining and gracious company. This book seems much like a well-executed banquet to me, and I would like to express my appreciation to all who made it possible.

As owners of the Cakewalk, the Gallaghers so graciously offered the opportunity for culinary excellence, a unique breadth of experience, along with a desire for quality that remains a driving force behind every project at his helm. The Gallaghers offered great support and hospitality as they opened their world and their home for many of the beautiful table settings which grace the photos herein. Many thanks also to Peter Korth, and Martin Richardson for the many kindnesses which made our days a little lighter as we cooked, measured, designed, photographed and yes, fretted over the quality of our presentations.

The careful eye of photographer Joe Coca can be spotted here, in the poise of a flower, the light dazzling a dessert, and the energy that charms a glow out of every recipe. I am very grateful to my editor, Judith Durant who enabled me to extract and refine the very elements of my style, and somehow make my words reside on paper with grace and form. The design and layout of this volume has been rendered by the skillful touch of Keith Rosenhagen, whose attention to detail adds beauty to every page. And many thanks to Barbara Ciletti, who provided the creative focus for this project, while keeping us all on course. Everything you see here came to life through the inspiration and printing wizardry of Barry Hirschfeld and A.B. Hirschfeld Press.

Yes, this book is like a banquet—a buffet of talent, friendship and commitment to quality. And like a fine meal, I hope that it lingers in your thoughts for some time to come.

– Dirk De Cuyper

Introduction

Welcome to *Charting Culinary Courses.* The publication of this
book reflects a unique and very creative collaboration of interests.
As the super yacht Cakewalk neared completion in Amsterdam,
owners Charlie and Diane Gallagher shared their enthusiasm
with the professionals at Feadship while plotting new courses
for future guests. And in the process, they realized that yacht
chef Dirk De Cuyper harbors creativity that needs to be shared.
A culinary tome that reflects a zest for life at sea, along with
recipes that can be made at home, seemed the perfect venue.
As Feadship continued with the construction of Cakewalk,
a talented chef and his culinary expertise came to port for the
creation of this book.

This is a story that embraces the sunlight that bathes the
CôteD'Azur and nestles into the terrain of Provence. It reflects
the heart of a sensitive chef who practices French culinary
technique while creating healthy, memorable meals. It also
exudes a lack of pretense, which resides as an unmistakable
quality of Dirk's cuisine as well as his approach to life. From the
beginning of this project, his focus has rested upon a cookbook
that speaks to armchair travelers as well as those lucky enough
enjoy a meal aboard Cakewalk.

As you absorb a view of the ports that mark the Cakewalk's
course, you can also explore the recipes, and revel in Dirk's
descriptions of his markets, his friends, and his philosophy
about culinary endeavors. You'll discover a certain magic that
can only be found where a love of the sea and fine dining create
new horizons. Enjoy!

*Chef Dirk De Cuyper rests
at an overlook above the
Monaco harbor.*

Being a chef is a very social and artful profession.

Most everybody enjoys eating. But the life is not always as fun as you may think. Like any other job, it has its frustrating moments. Getting to that certain level comes only after a hard school, years of experience, and patience. The key to success is loving it and keeping it interesting. Being a chef is being proud of what you do and respecting the principles, even when it takes the guests only a half-hour to eat what took you hours to prepare. The reward is when a guest can eat, relax and enjoy an evening. And service is as important as the food and wine—together they make a perfect dining experience.

On the Cakewalk I came to a level that allowed me to start my own repertoire. My kitchen is my life, and working on this book made me realize I wouldn't wish for anything else. I welcome you to my table and hope you enjoy the food.

– *Dirk De Cuyper*

THE CHEF AND THE SEA

irk De Cuyper is a yacht chef. For the past
two years, he's worked aboard the Cakewalk, a 142-foot
vessel that has launched a bounty of adventure and
culinary delight at sea. More recently, it's been replaced
by the new super yacht Cakewalk, more than 204 feet in
length, and like the vessels before it, crafted in true
Feadship style. Most people would agree De Cuyper is in
an enviable position. After all, his office is a luxurious motor
yacht, and if he's on duty, it means he's sailing the
Mediterranean or the Caribbean. That is not to say he
doesn't work hard. He starts his day at six a.m. and often
doesn't quit until all the dishes are washed after the evening
meal and the galley is spotless and ready for the next
morning. But, if he gets tired of looking at pastry dough or
a big pot of fish stock, all he has to do is go on deck,
breathe in the salt air and relish the expanse of blue sea.

"If you stand on the aft deck at sunrise or sunset," he
says, "the water is beautiful. That's one of the best parts
of a long journey."

Chef Dirk stands by the food he's prepared for Showboats International's contest, "Concours des chefs."

Chef Dirk took first prize in the "Concours des chefs" with his recipe for oven-baked sea bass.

Anyone who has ever had to cook in a tiny apartment kitchen knows the kind of creative maneuvering required to function in cramped conditions. Chef Dirk, who enjoys making fresh bread, created a makeshift proofing box for dough by putting a tray of hot water in the bottom of the oven and sliding the dough in above it. When the microwave wasn't being used to pop popcorn, it conveniently held a stack of kitchen towels. The old galley had a salamander that would set off the fire alarm when he opened the refrigerator. The pans were too big for the rings on the stove. The exhaust system sucked in hot air from outside, which turned the galley into a sauna, but Dirk couldn't turn on the air conditioner because the draft would cool off the hot food.

Despite these challenges, he still managed to deliver scrumptious meals with exquisite presentations that appeared to have been assembled by a team of chefs. He continues to do that today in his new galley, which he helped to design so it's much easier for him to execute the wonderful Mediterranean-style meals he so enjoys preparing for guests.

THE CHEF AND THE LANDSCAPE

Architecture comes to life in the unique Provençal sunlight.

The French often use the term *coupe de parfums* on menus to describe a sampler plate of flavors. Along the Côte d'Azur, where the rocky beaches meet the jewel-toned Mediterranean, and the bouquets of lavender, olives in unlidded jars, and patches of wildflowers scent the breeze, you are unwittingly treated to an atmospheric coupe de parfums.

The effect of the Riviera is immediate. The light, which long has lured artists and sun worshippers, is impossibly more luminous than any other, bathing everything in the grace of its rays. The morning sun hits vine-covered walls, injecting vivacious energy into pale-blue wooden shutters and the serpentine greenness beneath them. That is the essence of Provence. The light is the mouth of a river that wends its way to the confluence of culture and cuisine, nature and art, history and the present, life and land.

This light is ever present in the Provençal palette of gold, blue, red, green, and lavender. The colors, bursting with absorbing intensity, display themselves in the linens and crafts

The harbor in Antibes is home to many small pleasure boats.

that line store windows. Hand-woven baskets tinted with Easter-egg shades sit in voluptuous stacks in doorways. Even a couple of ceramic flowerpots, one precariously balanced upon the other, can't escape the paintbrush.

The flow into Provençal cuisine is effortless. The food is not complicated. Cooks simply take advantage of the region's bounty and the lovely mix of culinary influences that meet in the Mediterranean. The produce is cause for celebration; markets teem with baskets of plump cherries, bright currants, raspberries, and *fraise de bois* ready for a juicy tart or simply to be enjoyed out of the carton. Berries are displayed in shallow, paper baskets, and the fruit are treated with care: Too much in a carton may cause bruising.

Sable-skinned fresh medjool dates, still attached to branches, release caramel sweetness with each bite. Cloth-lined bins of whole and ground spices sit in a patchwork, waiting for the inspired cook to scoop them up for a hearty daube or a bouillabaisse.

Typically, meats and seafood are grilled with olive oil and paired with a medley of vegetables or potatoes. *Rouget* (red mullet) and *loup de mer* (sea bass) are cooked whole, then boned at the table. Pepper steak is standard on menus. The garlicky, mayonnaise-like aioli usually accompanies a basket of bread. Fresh rosemary, fennel, thyme, and sage are plentiful. Tomatoes, artichokes, eggplants, and bell peppers easily commingle in ratatouille. And a dewy bottle of rosé is never far.

Dining *en plein air* completes a meal. It is only natural, after all, to be outside when the sun kisses the horizon. The café tables then begin to fill, mostly with vacationers, the effects of having spent a day in the sun apparent. Almost every home has a patio table and chairs. The last plates rarely are cleared before the stomach has had a chance to settle and the cheese tray has been given its due, which may be near midnight since dinner usually starts past eight or nine.

(top) Even the dinghies in Provence are brightly painted.

Hand-woven baskets such as these seen outside a shop in Antibes abound in Provence.

With the Provençal landscape as inspiration, Dirk plies his passion for cooking. An early love of food and restaurant dining led him to enroll in cooking school in his hometown of Antwerp, Belgium. He learned classical French cooking techniques during five years of study, and worked with master chefs who instilled discipline and tradition in his ethic.

He cooks Mediterranean style, using fresh, local, seasonal ingredients, but draws from his training in classical French cooking techniques. Understanding the principles that drive this chef offers insight to his brand of cuisine.

"I make everything from scratch. I try to be inventive with colors because I think colors are important: They have to match. The flavors have to blend in. There can't be too much salt, so I work a lot with fresh herbs. That way, the diner gets a nice scent before they taste. I like nice presentations that are simple and not bombastic. I don't like too much garnish or stuff you can't eat. Mint leaves, for example. I find them inedible. So, I try to have the colors, the flavors, the simplicity. That is the way it's supposed to be."

I grew up with asparagus. In Belgium, when the asparagus come out, people go to the restaurants for a kind of a festival. We always had Mechelaen asparagus, which is the most traditional type of asparagus. It was nice.

Often, the French term *terroir* is used in discussions about wine. Chef Dirk, however, emphasizes its importance in creating and providing unique dining experiences. Roughly defined, terroir means terrain or earth (soil) and the factors that affect the growing conditions. The word embraces the notion that every plot of land has its own composition of influences that culminate in the final product. This is why a wine made of Cabernet Sauvignon grapes from France's Bordeaux region tastes different from a California Cabernet Sauvignon.

Because of terroir, Dirk likes to shop locally in the ports the Cakewalk visits. He values the inherent characteristics and quality of the raw ingredients he finds in those locales. Freshness is the priority: Certainly, a basket of strawberries picked the same morning it is brought to the market by the farmer outside of town is more desirable than berries that had to travel across the country. He also enjoys showcasing regional specialties.

Chef Dirk lets the produce inspire each day's menu. If white asparagus are in season, they might serve as garnish for a plate of risotto or the base of a soup, which shows the sweet, earthy flavor particularly well. He may wrap spears in salmon or ham, or fry them to serve with grilled fish. The peelings from the stalks add another dimension to a vegetable stock. If the figs are extra plump, they might appear in a dessert sauce as an accompaniment to homemade ice cream, or in a terrine with foie gras.

The same quality principle applies to the meats and poultry served aboard the Cakewalk. Chef Dirk depends on the Au Boeuf Couronne butcher shop in Antibes to supply the yacht with the best meats available in the region. The beef is Limousin or Charolais, both considered the most tender and flavorful in France. The butcher also supplies Bresse poultry. The exception is lamb. Chef Dirk prefers Colorado lamb to any other, when he can get it. He believes the conditions under which the Colorado sheep are raised produces a flavor unmatched by any other.

With these ingredients, Chef Dirk fashions a culinary repertoire of complex flavor combinations as well as a collection of classic offerings executed to perfection. From his prolific toque, he pulls out such tantalizing dishes as oven-braised sea bass marinated in champagne and lavender served over sautéed fennel, and carpaccio of shrimp and scallops served in warm shrimp consommé enriched with mushroom, onion, cucumber, tomato, basil, and lemon zest. They are a mouthful to say, but the final product is nothing short of heavenly.

Chef Dirk believes in honest cooking. He could, for example, make Spanish paella. But he would never presume to call it "traditional" because there is a deep-seated history of making paella he has not been exposed to as a non-Spaniard. Again, the idea of terroir comes into play. Chef Dirk wants guests to have a seamless and pleasurable dining experience aboard the Cakewalk. He hopes he also imparts through his art an understanding of that art. Such passion, dedication and insistence on quality are why a meal on the Cakewalk is never just a meal. It is a level of service that comes from Chef Dirk's heart.

Wine and other local products enhance the experience for visitors and make good souvenirs.

I want to bring something other than just eating to the guests so they learn something, too.

The lush landscape of Provence offers exquisite vistas.

Vegetable stands like this one in St. Tropez are cause for celebration.

On this voyage, the Cakewalk sets sail for St. Tropez, Cannes, Antibes, Golfe Juan, Nice, and Monaco. Each port has a particular personality that must be experienced. Though the Cote d'Azur is not his birthplace, it has become Chef Dirk's home. He feels as much a part of the landscape as the quaint hill towns. When he is in port, he knows he belongs nowhere else. Chef Dirk infuses Provence in the atmosphere aboard the Cakewalk, making sure guests leave with a lasting impression of the visit. What he can't bring to the Cakewalk, he encourages guests to seek.

Often a memento, such as Provençal table linens, a woven market satchel, herb-flavored oils, or ceramic ware serves as a reminder. Admire a game of boules, eavesdrop on an animated discussion between two card players, breathe in the perfume of a grand bouquet of roses, or stop and have a beer at the pub. Make it a point to stop at the fruit stand or the cheese kiosk. The local farmers and shopkeepers are Chef Dirk's friends and, by extension, friends of the guests.

The Markets

One of the immense pleasures of visiting France is attending the fresh markets. The produce is unquestionably fresh, the meat cut to order, the bread warm from the oven, the cheese artisanal. Chef Dirk regularly visits the markets early in the morning, when he is the most creative, allowing freshness and seasonality to dictate the course of the day's menu.

The flower market in Nice is unparalleled in the world.

The market in St. Tropez sits in a hidden square a few minutes walk from the frenzy of yachts and a sailboats. After selecting a mix of fresh fruit, we come upon an assortment of olives that call to be served as a snack. Fuchsia and pale pink peonies will make a lovely arrangement for the breakfast table.

In Cannes, Fourville market has almost as many fresh flower stands as produce stands. The banquet table of dried herbs and spices is difficult to ignore. The asparagus looks ripe for serving, perhaps in that risotto dish. And the strawberries are perfect for a tart.

The Antibes market bustles with activity. One stand offers homemade spreads and honey, each lovingly packaged in a hand-decorated jar. The market is adjacent to an old church, where on this day, a wedding is in progress. We can't be late for this market, though, because in the afternoon, the canopy shelters parked cars.

The Nice market is known for its garden of flower stands. It is brimming with everything from daisies and roses to hibiscus and lilies. There is a stand offering a rainbow of mini marzipan fruits and vegetables much too pretty to eat. Before grabbing a quick bite at one of the dozens of outdoor cafés, Chef Dirk decides on a large bouquet of spring flowers to add some cheer to the day.

The fresh vegetables at the markets dictate Chef Dirk's daily menus.

Dirk and the butcher take
time to catch up on life
and conduct business over
espresso and croissants.

Dirk buys most of his
meat from Jean-Raymond
Massenet in Antibes.

J ean-Raymond Massenet and his wife have been running
the Au Boeuf Couronne butcher shop in Antibes for ten
years. The couple and their two children previously lived in
Cannes, but have found home here. "Antibes is much more
convivial," he says in typical lightening-speed French. "Here,
we take the time to live."

Jean-Raymond also takes the time to conduct business,
usually over espresso and a chocolate croissant at the café
next door to his shop. That's where Chef Dirk and he talk
about the latest meat order and catch up on life. It's also
where I met this cheerful butcher who doesn't mince
words when it comes to meat: French cows, especially the
Limousin and the Charolais, are the best. The French
meatpacking industry is heavily controlled against the use
of hormones and chemicals. If handlers do not comply with
government regulations they could face jail.

The lifestyle and the mentality of the people who live in this area lured Jean-Raymond away from his birthplace in the Loire. "I like the beautiful region, the sun, the extraordinary Provençal cuisine, the beaches, the herbs—it's fabulous. I am in love with the Côte d'Azur."

A Special Place

Chef Dirk holds St. Paul-de-Vence, just north of Cannes, dear to his heart. Centuries-old buildings extend over labyrinthine walkways. Artists inhabit the town, and almost every doorway opens to a gallery. The town offers a refuge from the frenetic pace of his world. "The place gives you a good feeling in your heart. It opens your mind to the idea that there's something else in life."

It is the beauty of St. Paul-de-Vence that Chef Dirk expresses in his cooking. He conveys what he sees with his eyes and senses with his soul in the dishes he creates. If he could prepare a plate to represent St. Paul-de-Vence, he would make various vegetable confits and arrange them in dollops in a soup bowl. He then would add a skimming of fresh consommé, seasoned with fresh herbs, and served chilled. Because it's a mountainous area, Chef Dirk would serve lamb, thinly sliced. The color tones would be muted to match the rustic color of the old stone buildings and the land. "I want to show people this beauty with my cooking and tell them why food is done the way it's done."

Colors create flavors, flavors create taste.

Dirk is in his element when surrounded by the Provençal sun and sea.

St. Paul-de-Vence is Dirk's favorite place, and he visits at least two or three times a season.

A SPECIAL TOUCH

THEORY AND MEASUREMENTS

Cooking is an art, and as such is open to personal expression and interpretation. It is in that spirit that these recipes are presented. They are meant to serve as guidelines for your own taste, not as scientific formulas. If a recipe calls for an herb that you don't like, don't use it! You can either eliminate the ingredient or experiment with substitutes until you find one that works. The recipes will make six servings unless otherwise indicated.

Many of the recipes call for inexact amounts, to be adjusted for your personal preference. The amounts can loosely be interpreted as follows.

Dollop Similar to a spoonful, usually used for a creamy ingredient such as butter.

Glass This is the amount of liquid that can be held in a small juice glass.

Handful Usually used for chopped herbs or vegetables, it's what you can comfortably pick up in one hand without using the other to pack it in.

Ladle A liquid measure, it's just that—a soup ladleful.

Pinch The amount of dry ingredient, usually ground, that you can pick up between your thumb and forefinger.

Splash From a bottle with a large, unobstructed opening, the amount of liquid that comes out when you turn the bottle over and count to one. From a bottle with a spout (such as many vinegar bottles), it's the amount that comes out with three or four shakes of the bottle.

Spoonful A wet or dry measurement, it's about what fits in the spoon you set your table with, somewhere between an American teaspoon and tablespoon.

Once you've prepared the food to your satisfaction, remember that the right atmosphere is crucial to a successful dining experience. Do not stint when it comes to china, linens, flowers, and other table accessories. Your guests should be treated to complete sensory delight; sight and sound are as important as smell and savor.

To guide your guests, you may explain your food and the choices you made. But don't overdo this—just a little too much will be very annoying. Learn about wine, and choose specifically for the cuisine.

The more attention you pay to the details of food presentation, the more favorably memorable your table will be. Bon Appétit!

The stocks, or fonds, that follow are the basis for all soups and sauces but are also used for lamb, veal, and duck au jus. Simply use the stock in place of water in preparations to intensify the flavor. For white stocks of any other meat, follow the same process as for white beef stock.

basics.

Fond Brun or Beef Stock

This is the quantity I make to have on hand. You may freeze
half for later use or make half the recipe.
10 kilos (22 pounds) beef bones
6 whole carrots
4 whole onions
¼ head celery
2 tins tomato paste
water
salt, black peppercorns, laurel, and thyme

Roast bones in oven until golden brown. Add vegetables
to the bones and top with tomato paste. Leave in the
oven for ½ to 1 hour more.

Remove from oven and put everything into a pot. Add
water to cover. Bring to a fast boil, then reduce heat. Add
seasonings to taste. Slow cook for 6 hours. Strain and cool.

Fond Blanc or White Beef Stock

Again, this is the quantity I make to have on hand. You may
freeze half for later use or make half the recipe.
10 kilos (22 pounds) beef bones
10 whole carrots
5 whole onions
10 clove stems
½ bunch parsley
water
salt, black peppercorns, laurel, and thyme

To remove blood and open the pores of the bones, place
them in a pot, cover with cold water, and add a handful of
salt. Bring to a fast boil, then rinse the bones with fresh
cold water.

Put the clean bones in a pot. Add vegetables, cloves, and
parsley. Cover with cold water, bring to a fast boil, then
reduce heat. Add salt, peppercorns, laurel, and thyme.
Leave for six hours on slow cook. Strain and cool.

Fish Stock

This stock is made of fish bones, skin, and heads. Not all fish are good for this preparation. I recommend sole, turbot, or snapper—these are very white fish with fresh flavor and will create a clear stock.

1 spoonful chilled butter

1 kilo (about 2 ¼ pounds) fish bones, skin, and heads

4 carrots, chopped coarse

3 onions, chopped coarse

½ liter (about 2 ¼ cups) white cooking wine

water

salt and black peppercorns

Smear the bottom of a wide round pot with butter. Add the fish, vegetables, and wine. Add water to cover. Bring to a boil, then reduce heat. Add salt and peppercorns to taste. Slow cook for 30 to 40 minutes. Strain carefully and cool.

Chicken Stock

2 whole chickens

6 carrots, chopped coarse

4 onions, studded with cloves from 8 stems

½ head celery, chopped coarse

water

salt, black peppercorns, laurel, and thyme

Put chicken, and chopped vegetables in pot. Add water to cover. Bring to a boil, then reduce heat to low. Add seasonings to taste. Slow cook for about 4 hours.

Sauce Aigre Doux

This is a sweet-and-sour sauce that I use with duck and other meat dishes. This is unlike the Chinese sweet-and-sour sauce you may know—it is made with beef stock.

1 handful sugar
splash of white vinegar
1 glass orange or other fruit juice
2 ladles beef stock
seasonings to taste

Heat sugar in a small pot over high heat until caramelized. Douse with vinegar carefully because it will spit out of the pot. Add fruit juice and blend. Drown with beef stock. Reduce heat and cook over low heat until thickened. Season to taste.

Sauce Bordelaise

This is a basic red wine sauce that I use for various meat and fish preparations, and coq au vin.

2 shallots, chopped
1 glass red Bordeaux
2 ladles beef stock
seasonings to taste

Place shallots and wine in small pot over high heat and bring to a boil. Drown with beef stock. Reduce heat and cook over low heat until thickened. Season to taste.

Beurre Manié

I use this paste to thicken sauces and soups. Make whatever quantity you want using the following proportions.
⅔ flour
⅓ chilled butter

Make paste of the flour and butter. Add by dollop to sauce until you get the desired thickness.

Sometimes the effort you put into a dish is the main ingredient for success. The product may not work out, but it's the effort and the heart behind the meal that counts.

Baking on a boat is very different from working in the bakery where I learned the importance of good freshly made bread. But over time I came to a recipe that works in every situation, and I can change the flavor on a daily basis in order to keep up with the guests. I can also change the flavor to use ingredients at hand. For instance, if there is leftover bacon from breakfast, I use it to make bacon buns. Only one rule applies: Always add your flavoring ingredients to the flour before you add the water and yeast.

breads

Basic Dough

1 packet dried yeast

300 milliliters (about 10 fluid ounces) water

500 grams (3 ¾ cups) flour

2 pinches salt

Place the yeast in a small bowl and cover with a bit of the water. Let stand for about 10 minutes. Put the flour in a large mixing bowl and add salt. Add remaining water to yeast, then add mixture to flour. Mix and form into a ball. Cover with a kitchen towel and set aside in a warm area to rise for about 2 hours until doubled in size.

Tomato Foccacia

1 recipe Basic Dough

2 tomatoes, peeled, seeded, and chopped

2 cloves garlic, chopped fine

2 spoonfuls tomato sauce

a few drops of olive oil

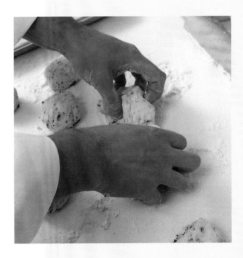

Prepare Basic Dough as described above, adding the tomatoes, garlic, and tomato sauce to the flour and mixing well. Add the olive oil to the flour mixture with the yeast and water. Mix thoroughly and form into a ball. Cover with a kitchen towel and place in a warm area to rise.

When the dough has doubled in size, place it on a work surface and form into 2 balls. Roll them out and put them into 2 omelette pans. Be sure to use omelette pans with ovenproof handles, and always butter and dust the pan with flour to prevent the bread from sticking. Cover with a kitchen towel and set in a warm place for 20 minutes. Remove the towel and punch holes in the dough, wetting your fingers with water to keep the dough from sticking. Sprinkle olive oil over the dough and spread it throughout the dough without pressing. Sprinkle with salt.

Bake at 205°C (400°F) for about 15 to 20 minutes. To create steam in the oven, chuck in a small handful of water and quickly close the door. The steam will help keep the bread moist while baking.

Remove the pan and put it on a wire rack. Unlike other breads, foccacia should be cooled in the pan so it retains the oil and doesn't dry out.

Variations

Prepare Basic Dough as described on page 31, add any of the flavorings listed here to the flour, and mix well before adding the yeast and water. Mix thoroughly and form into a ball. Cover with a kitchen towel and place in a warm area to rise. When the dough has doubled in size, place it on a work surface. Now you may prepare it in several ways for baking.

Regular Loaf

Shape the dough into a loaf and place it in a greased and floured loaf pan. Cover with a kitchen towel and put aside in a warm place to rise again. Bake at 205°C (400°F) for about 15 to 20 minutes. Remove loaf from pan and place on wire rack to cool.

Mini Loaves

Cut the dough into 6 equal portions. Knead each portion into a small ball. Shape the balls into small loaves and place in greased and floured mini loaf pans. Cover with a kitchen towel and put aside in a warm place to rise again. Bake at 205°C (400°F) for about 15 to 20 minutes. Remove loaves from pans and place on wire rack to cool.

Buns

Divide the dough into 10 to 12 equal portions. Knead each portion into a small ball. Place the balls on a greased and floured baking sheet. Cover with a kitchen towel and put aside in a warm place to rise again. Bake at 205°C (400°F) for about 15 to 20 minutes. Remove buns from pan and place on wire rack to cool.

flavor variations

Olive Bread

300 grams (10 ½ ounces) black olives, pitted and chopped

Basil Bread

2 cloves garlic, chopped fine

1 small onion, chopped fine

1 small handful basil leaves, chopped fine

Sweet Corn Bread

1 small tin sweet corn

Sundried Tomato and Pine Nut Bread

200 grams (7 ounces) sundried tomatoes, chopped

200 grams (7 ounces) pine nuts

Dill and Feta Bread

200 grams (7 ounces) feta cheese, cubed

1 handful dill, chopped fine

Butter Croissants

■

560 grams (4 ¼ cups) flour

1 handful sugar

3 pinches salt

275 grams (9 ½ ounces) chilled butter

1 packet dry yeast

240 milliliters (about 8 fluid ounces) milk

180 milliliters (about 6 fluid ounces) water

Place flour, sugar, salt, and 25 grams (⅞ ounce) of the butter in a mixing bowl. Work the butter into the dry ingredients.

Mix in the yeast, milk, and water. Make into a ball and put in refrigerator under plastic film for up to 2 hours, until the dough has risen a little. Place it on a floured work surface and let the dough get to room temperature. Roll out onto a floured surface into a rectangular shape. Add the remaining butter down the center of the dough and fold dough in thirds, making one layer over the butter, the other over the dough. Place it in a plastic bag in refrigerator for 10 minutes. Repeat the rolling and layering process 2 more times without adding butter.

Return dough to refrigerator and leave for 2 hours. Roll out again and form your croissants.

Danish Pastry

560 grams (4 ½ cups) flour

1 handful sugar

3 pinches salt

3 pinches cardamom

275 grams (9 ½ ounces) chilled butter

1 packet dry yeast

240 milliliters (about 8 fluid ounces) milk

180 milliliters (about 6 fluid ounces) water

1 egg, beaten

Place flour, sugar, salt, cardamom, and 25 grams (⅞ ounce) of the butter in a mixing bowl. Work the butter into the ingredients.

Dissolve the yeast in the milk and water. Add the beaten egg and mix well, then add to flour and butter mixture. Make into a ball and put in refrigerator under plastic film for up to 2 hours, until the dough has risen a little. Place it on a floured work surface and let the dough get to room temperature. Roll out onto a floured surface into a rectangular shape. Add the remaining butter down the center of the dough and fold dough in thirds, making one layer over the butter, the other over the dough. Place it in a plastic bag in refrigerator for 10 minutes. Repeat the rolling and layering process 2 more times without adding butter.

Return dough to refrigerator and leave for 2 hours. Roll out again and form your Danish.

Danish pastry is prepared the same way as croissant dough with the addition of cardamom and egg.

Pâte Brisée

◼

500 grams (3 ¾ cups) flour
300 grams (10 ½ ounces) chilled butter
200 milliliters (about 7 fluid ounces) water

Mix flour with butter and water in a small bowl. Form into a ball and refrigerate for 2 hours. Remove and let the dough reach room temperature. Roll out and use.

Puff Pastry

◼

500 grams (3 ¾ cups) flour
2 pinches salt
500 grams (17 ½ ounces) butter
300 milliliters (about 10 fluid ounces) water

Place flour, salt, and 50 grams (2 ounces) of the butter in a mixing bowl and work the butter into the dry ingredients. Add the water and form a ball. Refrigerate for 10 to 15 minutes.

Remove from refrigerator and roll out on a floured surface into a rectangular shape. Add the remaining butter down the center of the dough and fold dough in thirds, making one layer over the butter, the other over the dough. Place it in a plastic bag in refrigerator for 10 minutes. Repeat the rolling-out and folding process two more times without adding butter.

I use pâte brisée or puff pastry for tart bottoms and pies. The pâte brisée is crusty, while the puff pastry is flakier and quicker to bake.

Lunchtime on the Cakewalk is around 2 p.m. The yacht is usually on anchor, and the guests are relaxing in the sun or using the water toys. Because it is quite hot and sunny, I serve three or four different salads, which are light, with a grilled fish or meat preparation. The lunch is served Russian style, so the guests may take what they choose.

I make salads with both raw vegetables and poached vegetables that have been cooled down. My dressings often contain chopped fruits, nuts, or seafood, and I almost always add chopped parsley.

For most salads, the dressing may be added and left to sit for a while. However, if you are using lettuce, add the dressing just before serving—lettuce tends to go flat when the dressing sits on it too long.

salads

Salad of Tomato, Black Olive, Red Onion, and Watercress

5 tomatoes, peeled and sliced into 6 pieces each
1 handful black olives, pitted and sliced thin
1 red onion, sliced very thin
½ bunch parsley, chopped
1 bunch watercress, leaves only
2 cloves garlic, chopped fine
salt and pepper
30 milliliters (1 fluid ounce) red wine vinegar
90 milliliters (3 fluid ounces) walnut oil

Combine tomatoes, olives, onion, parsley, and watercress in a salad bowl. Add garlic and salt and pepper to taste. Add the vinegar and oil and toss well. Cover the salad with plastic film and refrigerate for at least 2 hours before serving.

For using tomatoes in salads, I recommend peeling them. (See instructions on page 57.) Tomato skins have a bitter taste, and when they are removed, the flesh will absorb the flavor of the dressing. Tomato salads go quite well with almost any meat.

Julienne Vegetables in Mustard, Honey, Dill, and Garlic Dressing

200 grams (7 ounces) pumpkin
200 grams (7 ounces) celery
1 onion
1 head Belgian endive
Honey-Mustard Dressing (see recipe below)
¼ head iceberg lettuce

Julienne the pumpkin, celery, onion, and endive. Mix them together and add dressing. Julienne the iceberg lettuce and mix into salad when ready to serve.

Honey-Mustard Dressing
2 spoonfuls Dijon mustard, with seeds
1 spoonful liquid honey
1 clove garlic, chopped fine
3 spoonfuls dill, chopped fine
60 milliliters (about 2 fluid ounces) olive oil
splash of red wine vinegar

Mix the mustard, honey, garlic, and dill. Drizzle the olive oil into the mixture and whisk to blend well. Add vinegar.

This salad shows off the color and structure of the vegetables. I serve this tender salad with white meat, poultry, or fish. You could also marinate a chicken breast in the dressing and grill or panfry it and serve it with the salad.

Poached Broccoli Florets with
Pecan Caesar Dressing

2 heads broccoli

1 handful pecan nuts, chopped fine

2 spoonfuls parsley, chopped fine

2 spoonfuls mustard

1 clove garlic, chopped fine

3 anchovy fillets

pepper

160 milliliters (about 5 ½ fluid ounces) olive oil

80 milliliters (about 3 fluid ounces) red wine vinegar

splash of balsamic vinegar

1 spoonful dill, chopped fine

4 spoonfuls Parmesan, grated

shredded Parmesan for garnish

Remove broccoli florets from the stems. Poach them in boiling water for 5 to 6 minutes. Run them under cold water immediately, and continue flushing until the florets are cold— this will stop the cooking process. Put the broccoli in a salad bowl; add pecans and parsley and mix.

Prepare the dressing in a food processor. Start with the mustard, garlic, anchovy, and pepper. Add olive oil and red wine vinegar and blend. Pour into a small bowl. Add balsamic vinegar, dill, and grated Parmesan. Adjust oil and vinegar to taste.

Add the dressing to the broccoli mix and toss well. Garnish with shredded Parmesan.

Many raw vegetables can be bitter and hard. Poaching brings out both the color and flavor of broccoli. This technique is also successful with cauliflower, carrots, and celery. Simply poach, cool, and serve cold.

White Cabbage with Cilantro, Chicken, Mango, and Walnuts

■

2 boneless, skinless chicken breasts
splash of olive oil
3 blood oranges
1 spoonful mustard
1 spoonful tequila
80 milliliters (about 3 fluid ounces) red wine vinegar
1 mango, very ripe, peeled, deseeded, and diced
salt and pepper
160 milliliters (about 5 ½ fluid ounces) olive oil
1 head white cabbage, shredded
1 spoonful cilantro, chopped fine
1 small handful walnuts, chopped

Slice the chicken into splinter-thin strips and marinate in a little olive oil, the juice of one orange, salt, and pepper. Let sit for about 15 minutes. Panfry chicken in a very hot pan to sear and set aside.

Prepare the dressing in a blender. Combine mustard, juice of 2 oranges, tequila, red wine vinegar, and half the mango. Start blending and add salt and pepper. Continue to blend, drizzling in the oil.

Combine the chicken, cabbage, remaining mango, cilantro, and walnuts. Add vinaigrette and toss. Salt and pepper to taste.

Here I've mixed a salad of vegetables with chicken. You can also use seafood or meat. In general, fruits go better with meat and poultry than with fish. Prepare meats separately and let them cool for several minutes before combining them with raw vegetables. The cilantro could be changed to dill or fennel greens, for example, allowing you to alter the recipe to personal taste or for available herbs.

Lobster Salad with Avocado, Yellow Beans, and Red Onions

2 cooked lobsters

100 grams (3 ½ ounces) yellow beans

1 red onion, sliced very fine

1 spoonful mustard

salt and pepper

juice of 1 lemon

2 pinches ground cumin

6 fresh mint leaves, chopped fine

80 milliliters (about 3 fluid ounces) white wine vinegar

160 milliliters (about 5 ½ fluid ounces) olive oil

1 ripe avocado

Cut the lobster meat into small cubes. Clean the beans, remove the ends, and blanch in boiling water until cooked al dente. Run them under cold water immediately, and continue flushing until the beans are cold—this will stop the cooking process.

Combine the lobster, beans, and onion in a salad bowl and set aside.

Prepare the dressing in a blender. Combine mustard, salt and pepper, lemon juice, cumin, mint, and white wine vinegar. Blend well. While continuing to blend, drizzle in the olive oil.

Just before serving, peel the avocado, remove the pit, and slice into cubes. Add this to the lobster mixture. Add the dressing and toss. Adjust seasoning to taste.

This salad uses several different types of ingredients and preparations. The lobsters are cooked and then peeled, preserving the flavor. The beans are poached and cooled. The onion and avocado are left raw and cut into julienne and cubes. The dressing has a Mediterranean flavor, with scents that remind me of Morocco.

Shrimp Salad with Bisque Parmesan Dressing

½ kilo (about 1 pound) large shrimp

splash of olive oil

1 spoonful cognac

240 milliliters (about 8 fluid ounces) lobster bisque

2 tomatoes, peeled

100 grams (3 ½ ounces) bean sprouts

1 bunch watercress

1 spoonful mustard

1 spoonful grated Parmesan

1 spoonful olive oil

splash of red wine vinegar

2 spoonfuls chopped parsley

shredded Parmesan for garnish

Peel the shrimp, remove the heads, and devein. Sauté the peels and heads in a pot of hot olive oil. Add cognac, then lobster bisque. If necessary, thin with a little water. Cook until well blended and reduced. Strain and cool. Set aside for dressing.

Slice the shrimp in half lengthwise. Panfry, then cool. Quarter the tomatoes, seed, and dice. Blanche the bean sprouts for about 1 minute. Run them under cold water immediately, and continue flushing until the sprouts are cold—this will stop the cooking process. Remove the watercress leaves from the stems.

To make the vinaigrette, add the mustard, Parmesan, and olive oil to the cooled bisque mixture. Add red wine vinegar.

Combine the shrimp, tomatoes, bean sprouts, watercress, and parsley in a salad bowl. Add the dressing and toss. Garnish with shredded Parmesan.

Here again I prepare the shrimp separately from the vegetables. Shrimp are soft and light in flavor, so I like to combine them with tender vegetables like lettuce, bean sprouts, and watercress. This salad is designed to use up leftover Lobster Bisque (see page 63).

*N*o matter what the course, I feel it is important that the guest notice the thought and effort that went into it. Soups offer lots of room for creativity, and I serve them both hot and cold. And because I tend to be classic with main courses, I like being a bit extravagant in the presentation of starters. Just be careful not to plate up too high—tumbled food is very unappealing.

soups *and* starters

Terrine of Tomato, Mozzarella, and Basil

6 tomatoes, peeled and sliced
salt and pepper
2 cloves garlic, chopped fine
1 small handful basil leaves, chopped fine
olive oil
balsamic vinegar
red wine vinegar
3 buffalo mozzarella, sliced

To make the tomatoes easy to peel, dip them into boiling water for about 10 seconds, then run them under cold water. Remove the skin and cut fruit into 4 or 5 slices. Lay the slices out on a flat tray and sprinkle with salt and pepper. Add chopped garlic and basil. Drizzle with olive oil and vinegar. Do not drown the tomatoes, but add just enough liquid to thoroughly coat them. Toss carefully until everything is evenly divided. Cover with plastic film and refrigerate for a couple of hours.

Line one terrine pot with plastic film, leaving enough extra on one side to cover the top once it is filled. Place one layer of tomatoes in the terrine. Use only what you need for a single layer to make sure you have enough for the entire terrine. Cover the tomatoes with a layer of sliced mozzarella. Continue layering in this manner until the terrine is filled. Use the remaining marinade as a dressing when serving.

Cover the terrine with plastic film and place on a tray. Fill the second terrine with water and place on top of the filled terrine. Refrigerate the tray of terrines overnight. Some of the liquid marinade will ooze from the terrine and be caught in the tray to protect your refrigerator.

Remove the tray from the refrigerator and take the water-filled terrine off the other. Uncover the filled terrine and turn it out onto a cutting board, removing the plastic film. Slice the terrine into 10 to 13 pieces. To serve, place one portion in the center of a plate and drizzle marinade around the serving.

To make terrines, I use two terrine pots and a technique called *en presse*. The first terrine pot is filled with the ingredients, and the second is filled with water and placed on top of the first. The pots are then refrigerated overnight. The ingredients become pressed together into a solid mass, which can be removed from the pot and sliced.

Here I use the technique with traditional ingredients. After coming up with this dish, I went on a terrine binge and made a few different ones every day for a week. Not all things are suitable for this preparation—soft ingredients make cutting much easier.

Porridge of Carrots, Potatoes, and Sundried Tomatoes

10 large carrots, chopped coarse

5 potatoes, peeled and cubed

splash of olive oil

200 grams (7 ounces) sundried tomatoes, chopped

2 liters (about 2 ¼ quarts) White Beef or Chicken Stock
    (see pages 24 and 25)

1 bunch chives, chopped

Put the carrots, potatoes, and olive oil in a large pot over medium heat. Cover and cook for about 15 minutes. The lid is important for creating steam, which makes the vegetables sweat and keeps them from drying out. Add the sundried tomatoes and cook for another 10 to 15 minutes, occasionally stirring with a wooden spoon to prevent the vegetables from darkening and becoming bitter. Add stock and cook for 30 to 45 minutes. Blend the soup with a wand-type soup mixer. Let the soup cool. Add chives before serving. For soup, thin with cream, milk, Madeira, or water.

This porridge is a thick variation of vichyssoise, which is usually made with leeks and potatoes. Here I substitute carrots for the leeks and add sundried tomatoes, which create a rich flavor and color.

I made this porridge while in Italy to serve one late afternoon to guests who had been out on an excursion. Served cold, it makes a fresh, light, and healthy snack. Do keep in mind that what you prepare hot and serve cold tends to lose flavor, so season well when preparing. Add salt while the soup is hot to keep it from crystallizing.

Lamb Consommé with Sage, Lavender, and Madeira

10 large carrots, cubed

4 celery stalks, cubed

1 leek, cubed

200 grams (about ½ pound) ground lamb

3 sage leaves, chopped fine

1 spoonful lavender

1 tin tomato paste

½ liter (about 2 ¼ cups) egg whites

5 liters (about 5 ½ quarts) lamb stock
    (lamb bones cooked in white stock or water)

1 glass Madeira

sage for garnish

This classic brew could be called the royalty of soups. Its strong flavor and tradition add an ageless touch to any menu, and you will often find it on a European bill of fare for a Christmas or New Year's dinner. It requires quite a long time to prepare, but the result is well worth the effort.

Preparing the clarif

Clarif is made with egg whites and is used to clarify a stock. It will create a golden transparent bouillon, which is then called consommé. Place the carrots, celery, and leek in a mixing bowl. Add the ground lamb, sage, lavender, and tomato paste. Mix well and add the egg whites. Mix thoroughly, cover with plastic film, and refrigerate, not more than 1 hour, while you prepare the stock.

Preparing the consommé

Pour the lamb stock and Madeira into a tall pot. Bring to a fast boil, add the clarif, and stir. Reduce heat and stir once more, just to circulate the stock. Cook on low boil so the stock continues to circulate. The clarif will float, absorb the fat, and clarify the stock. Cook on low heat for 3 hours. You may adjust the seasoning during this 3-hour period—but once the stock is done, flavors will no longer blend.

Strain the stock through a sieve and cheesecloth. You should now have a clear golden consommé. Once the consommé has been strained, do not reboil. To serve, add some shredded lamb and perhaps some cubed tomatoes. Garnish with sage.

Lobster Bisque

2 live Maine lobsters

splash of olive oil

2 spoonfuls ginger, chopped

3 carrots, chopped

2 onions, chopped

½ glass cognac

2 spoonfuls flour

2 spoonfuls tomato paste

4 liters (about a gallon) fish stock

1 handful cilantro, chopped

240 milliliters (about 1 cup) cream

Cut the live lobsters in half lengthwise. Heat the olive oil in a tall pot and add the lobsters with 1 spoonful of the chopped ginger. Sauté until the color changes to orange. Add the carrots and onions and sauté for a few more minutes. Add the cognac and blend. Add flour, tomato paste, and stir. Add the fish stock, stir well, and bring to a boil. Reduce heat to low and slow cook for 4 hours.

Strain the soup through a chinois, pressing the lobster meat against the sides and squeezing out the juice. Finish the bisque with the cream, chopped cilantro, a spoonful of chopped ginger, and perhaps more cognac to taste. Add some cooked lobster to the soup if desired.

SOUPS AND STARTERS

Here is another classic and celebrated soup, one found on menus for wedding parties and other special events. While I think of consommé as having a male character, I find bisque more female in nature.

Red Snapper with Ginger, Orange, and Basil

6 boneless pieces of red snapper—
    100 – 120 grams
    (about 4 ounces) each
1 orange
1 spoonful ginger, chopped
4 leaves basil, chopped
salt and pepper
3 heads Belgian endive

olive oil
1 pinch ground ginger
1 spoonful plus 1 pinch sugar
2 bunches watercress, leaves only
splash of white vinegar
1 glass orange juice
1 glass beef stock
butter

Here I start with sweet orange basil sauce, and by adding ginger and using it with fish, I create a new relationship between sweet and salt. The somewhat bitter endive and watercress will complement the sweet sauce, and the combination is a perfect balance of flavor and color.

Preparing the fish
Arrange the fish in a flat tray. Squeeze the juice from the orange out over the fish and top with the ginger and three-fourths of the basil. Sprinkle with salt and pepper. Cover with plastic film and marinate in the refrigerator for 1 hour.

Preparing the salad
Cut the endive in half lengthwise. Remove and discard the heart, which is bitter. Julienne the endive. Lightly sauté it in olive oil, adding a pinch of salt, pepper, ginger, and sugar. Remove from pan and place in mixing bowl. Add watercress and toss.

Preparing the sauce
In a small saucepan, caramelize a spoonful of sugar. When the sugar is brown, add the vinegar, then the orange juice. Be careful when adding the liquids because the heat will cause them to be spit from the pan. Lower the heat and cook until sugar is dissolved. Add the stock and reduce until the sauce is well blended and thickened.

Finishing
Melt butter in sauté pan and panfry the fish on both sides. Place endive and watercress salad in center of plate and put one piece of fish on top. Add remaining basil to the warm sauce and drizzle around the plate.

Tart of Dolphin, Spinach, Eggplant, and Tomato

6 pieces dolphin, 100 – 120
  grams (about 4 ounces) each

salt and pepper

splash of olive oil

6 handfuls raw spinach,
  well cleaned

1 eggplant, peeled and diced

7 tomatoes, peeled, seeded,
  and diced

splash of white wine

splash of white vinegar

3 ladles beef stock

1 spoonful parsley, chopped

1 spoonful chives, chopped

Here I use the word tart to indicate a layered preparation that is cooked in the oven. Layers of fish and vegetables are prepared as individual servings, keeping the fish juicy and full of flavor. Color is important in this dish, so I add fresh parsley and chives to the sauce at the end so they will stay nice and green.

Preparing the fish

Cut each piece of dolphin lengthwise into 3 thin fillets. Dry on paper towels and sprinkle with salt and pepper.

Sauté the spinach in olive oil until limp. Cool down. Sauté the eggplant until soft. Lightly sauté 6 of the tomatoes and mix with the eggplant.

Tear off 6 sheets of aluminum foil and brush with olive oil. Place 1 fillet on each piece of foil. To form each tart, put a spoonful of spinach on the fish, place a fillet over the spinach, put a spoonful of the eggplant and tomato mixture over the fish, and top with the remaining fillet. Add a little white wine to prevent the fish from drying out. Close the 6 foil packets and bake on a tray at 205°C (400°F) for 10 to 12 minutes.

Preparing the sauce

Sauté remaining tomato in a drop of vinegar. Add stock and season with salt and pepper.

Finishing

When fish is ready, open the foil and add the juice from the fish to sauce. Put some sauce in the middle of the plate and place the fish tart on top. Drizzle extra sauce on the plate and serve with the remaining eggplant and tomato mixture.

astas with tomato sauce can be filling, and are therefore difficult to incorporate into a dinner menu of several courses. They make excellent lunch dishes, and I also use ravioli or lasagna as a one-course dinner dish. These recipes use fish or seafood, poultry, or fowl. Most of the recipes call for a cream sauce; some use a classic tomato sauce, but I would serve these only for lunch.

I make my own pasta sheets for ravioli, lasagna, and tortellini, but I buy spaghetti, penne, and other pastas when I'm in Italy. The pastas I use are prepared with a unique drying process, which takes longer and uses less heat than most others do. They are made by the Latini company, a small family business. The result is pasta that is paler in color and richer in flavor.

pastas

Basic Pasta

This recipe is intended for use with a pasta machine. For basil, sundried tomato, or olive pastas, add these ingredients to the flour during preparation.

500 grams (3 ¾ cups) semolina flour
4 whole eggs
splash of olive oil
water

Place the flour and eggs in a food processor and mix well. Add a splash of olive oil and enough water to make the dough workable. Refrigerate for ½ hour.

Using a little flour to keep the dough from sticking, process dough through a pasta machine, forming thin sheets. Place the sheets on a floured surface and dry for 20 minutes.

Sauce Béchamel

This can serve as the base for a variety of cream sauces.

1 ¾ liters (about 2 quarts) milk
2 ¾ liters (about 3 quarts) veal stock
½ kilo (about 1 pound) Beurre Manié (see page 27)
salt, pepper, and nutmeg

Pour the milk and stock into a large pot and bring to a boil. Add dollops of beurre manié while stirring—this will keep the milk from burning and prevent lumps from forming. When all the manié has been added, stir for another 5 minutes and lower the heat.

Transfer the sauce to another container to cool, and season to taste. For example, to make a cheese sauce, add about 300 grams (10 ½ ounces) cheese to 1 liter (about 1 ¼ quarts) of sauce. Cooled béchamel is quite thick and may take awhile to reheat. To avoid burning it, add a splash of milk before reheating.

Basic Tomato Sauce

This is the basic tomato sauce I use for pastas. I also use it in other recipes.

4 cloves garlic

1 onion, chopped

olive oil

15 Roma tomatoes, peeled and chopped

½ liter (about 2 ¼ cups) veal stock

½ liter (about 2 ¼ cups) water

salt and pepper

1 pinch sugar

1 tin plump Roma tomatoes

2 tins tomato paste

In a wide pot, lightly sauté the garlic and onion in olive oil, making sure not to brown them. Add the fresh tomatoes and sauté for 5 to 10 minutes, stirring to avoid burning. Reduce heat and add the stock, water, salt and pepper, sugar, tinned tomatoes, tomato paste, and a splash of olive oil. Simmer for 30 to 45 minutes on low heat.

Spaghetti with Green Herbs and Scallops

500 grams (about 1 pound)
spaghetti
1 white onion, diced
½ liter (about 2 ¼ cups) fish stock
1 glass milk
1 spoonful Beurre Manié
   (see page 27)
salt, pepper, and nutmeg
2 egg yolks

120 milliliters
   (about 4 fluid ounces) cream
2 dozen scallops (4 per person)
splash of olive oil
1 handful parsley, chopped
1 handful chives, chopped
1 handful basil, chopped
1 avocado, diced
grated Parmesan for garnish

This preparation of spaghetti and panfried scallops is better suited to a main dinner course than to lunch. The fresh herbs give a special color to the dish and actually seem to lighten up the pasta itself.

Preparing the pasta
Cook pasta in boiling water, drain, and cool. Set aside until ready to serve.

Preparing the sauce velouté
Put the chopped onion and fish stock in a pot and bring to a boil. Cook for 5 minutes, then add milk and cook for another 5 minutes. Whisk in the beurre manié to slightly thicken the mixture. Season to taste with salt, pepper, and nutmeg.

Mix the egg yolks with the cream. To incorporate this into the sauce, pour a little sauce over the egg and cream mixture, blend well, then add this back into the sauce. Do not reboil the sauce or the eggs will scramble.

Finishing
Marinate the scallops in olive oil and a bit of the herbs. Panfry just before serving. Reheat the pasta and add half the sauce. Add remaining herbs and avocado and toss.

Serving
Put a large spoonful of sauce on a deep plate and cover with pasta. Place 3 scallops around the pasta, and put the fourth on top. Garnish with grated Parmesan.

Penne Pasta with Sundried Tomato and Eggplant

Although this is a somewhat filling pasta, it's one I like to serve for lunch. The sundried tomato and eggplant combine well with the tomato sauce.

500 grams (about 1 pound) penne pasta
2 eggplants, peeled and diced into small cubes
1 onion, chopped fine
olive oil
2 cloves garlic, chopped fine
2 handfuls sundried tomatoes, chopped
4 Roma tomatoes, peeled, seeded, and diced
3 ladles Basic Tomato Sauce (see page 71)
salt and pepper
1 handful parsley, chopped
1 handful basil, chopped

Bring water to a boil, add pasta, and cook until al dente. Drain, cool, and set aside until ready to serve.

Sauté the eggplant and onion in olive oil for 5 to 10 minutes, stirring continually with a wooden spoon to prevent burning. After 10 minutes, add the garlic and sundried tomatoes, cook 5 more minutes, then add the diced tomatoes.

Add the tomato sauce and some more olive oil, salt, and pepper, and simmer for ½ hour on low heat. Add herbs just before serving so they stay nice and green.

Reheat the pasta in a pan with a little olive oil. Place pasta in middle of plate and ladle the sauce on top.

Fettuccini Bagatelle

500 grams (about 1 pound) fettuccini
3 large portobello mushrooms, diced
1 fennel bulb, diced, with green removed, chopped, and set aside
olive oil
3 tomatoes, peeled, seeded, and diced
12 fillets red mullet (2 per person)
salt, pepper, and nutmeg
½ onion, chopped fine
1 glass white wine
1 ladle fish stock
200 milliliters (about 7 fluid ounces) cream
1 handful chopped parsley

Cook the pasta in boiling water, drain, and cool. Set aside
until ready to serve.

Sauté the diced mushrooms and fennel in a little olive oil,
stirring with a wooden spoon to avoid burning. Add the
tomatoes and sauté until tender.

Clean the fillets and remove the bones. Marinate in olive oil,
salt and pepper, and half of the fennel greens. Panfry just
before serving, skin side first.

Place the onion, white wine, and fish stock in a pot and
reduce. Add cream and reduce to a thickness that will coat
the back of a wooden spoon.

Add the sautéed vegetables to the sauce. Reheat the pasta
in a pan with a little olive oil, salt, pepper, and nutmeg. Add
chopped parsley and toss.

Put sauce on a deep plate, place pasta en dome on top of
sauce, and top with panfried fillets, skin side up.

Here I incorporate fish and a
cream sauce, and serve it as a
main course. The vegetables
add a gentle flavor. The
ingredients go very well with
the pasta, but they could
also be served on their own.

Lasagna of Salmon and Spinach

½ onion, chopped fine

1 glass white wine

240 milliliters (about 8 fluid ounces) fish stock

240 milliliters (about 8 fluid ounces) cream

1 spoonful chervil, chopped

1 regular or Roma tomato, peeled, seeded, and diced

1 recipe Basic Pasta dough (see page 70)
    with 3 minced garlic cloves added

½ side fresh boneless salmon, sliced thinly lengthwise

12 handfuls raw spinach, washed well

salt, pepper, and nutmeg

grated Parmesan for garnish

Place the onion, white wine, and fish stock in a pot and reduce. Add cream and reduce to a thickness that will coat the back of a wooden spoon. Add the chervil and tomato just before using.

Sauté spinach with salt, pepper, and nutmeg.

Put a ladle of sauce in the bottom of an 8 × 11 × 4-inch baking pan. Line the pan with one layer of pasta. Add a layer of half the salmon, sprinkle with salt and pepper, and cover with ½ ladle of sauce. Cover with a layer of pasta. Spread spinach evenly over pasta and cover with another sheet of pasta. Layer the remaining salmon, then the remaining pasta. Top with grated Parmesan and another half ladle of sauce.

Bake at 205°C (400°F) for 20 minutes, checking occasionally to make sure the top of the lasagna doesn't become dried out and crisp.

Serving
Place lasagna in center of plate and ladle sauce over the top. Garnish with Parmesan.

Here I change the classic preparation into a lighter dish by using a white sauce. I usually prepare this as a main course, but a small enough portion may also serve as an additional course on a menu.

Macaroni and Cheese Served with Quail Breasts

Here I used the idea of potato gratin to come up with a classic macaroni and cheese—the ingredients suit both potatoes and pasta. The cheese sauce combines well with the quail breasts.

1 liter (about 1 ¼ quarts) Sauce Béchamel (see page 70)

300 grams (10 ½ ounces) grated cheese

500 grams (about 1 pound) macaroni

6 handfuls spinach, washed well

salt, pepper, and nutmeg

18 quail breasts (3 per person)

1 spoonful thyme, chopped

juice of 1 lime

1 clove garlic, chopped fine

½ onion, chopped

5 fresh apricots, seeded and chopped

1 glass Madeira

2 ladles beef stock

1 handful pine nuts

Combine sauce béchamel and grated cheese. Cook the pasta in boiling water. Drain and mix with cheese sauce. Keep warm until ready to serve, but do not reboil.

Sauté the spinach with salt, pepper, and nutmeg.

Sprinkle quail breasts with thyme, salt, pepper, and lime juice; panfry shortly before serving.

Place the garlic, onion, and apricots in a saucepan with the wine and bring to a boil. Add the stock and reduce over lower heat to desired thickness. Add pine nuts and remaining lime marinade just before serving.

Serving
Spread sautéed spinach over plate. Add a serving of pasta and top with quail breasts. Nap (generously coat) sauce over the top and garnish with some chopped tomato or parsley, if desired.

Sheet Pasta with Shiitake Mushrooms, Leek, and Asparagus

■

Lasagna (1 sheet per person)
3 live Maine lobsters (½ per person)
1 spoonful cayenne pepper
splash of white cooking wine
1 whole leek, cut lengthwise into thin strips
½ bunch green asparagus, cut lengthwise into thin strips
1 handful shiitake mushrooms, cut into thin strips
½ onion, chopped fine
1 glass white wine
240 milliliters (about 8 fluid ounces) fish stock
240 milliliters (about 8 fluid ounces) cream
1 handful basil, chopped
grated Parmesan for garnish

Cook the pasta in boiling water. Drain, cool, and cut into desired shape.

Boil the lobsters in a large pot of water with cayenne pepper and cooking wine for approximately 8 minutes. Cool down and remove the meat from the tail, remove the bowel, and cut in half. Remove the claws from their shells.

Sauté the leek and asparagus in a wide pan. Sauté the mushrooms and add to the leek and asparagus.

Place the onion, white wine, and fish stock in a pot and reduce. Add cream and reduce to a thickness that will coat the back of a wooden spoon. Add basil.

Serving
Place some sauce on a plate. Make a bed of the vegetables, then place the lobster on the bed, then the pasta sheet over the lobster. Ladle sauce over the top. Garnish with Parmesan.

Here I make a lobster preparation and add a sheet of pasta on top. This has the effect of lasagna but is very light. The vegetables are cut into long julienne and serve as a bed for the lobster.

egetable preparations are needed to complete a dish. There are many ways to treat vegetables in classic French cuisine. While I'm not fond of plain steamed vegetables, I will prepare them on request. I prefer to prepare vegetables as gratin, glazed, pureed, or in some kind of sauce.

Vegetables prepared to accompany another food should be able to stand on their own as well. Keep an eye on the colors, and always keep in mind the season—buy only the best quality ripe vegetables.

Here are some preparations that can be used for a wide variety of vegetables and legumes.

vegetables

Sauté

This method involves lightly pan-frying in a little olive oil or butter, and is best used for vegetables that can be eaten raw, i.e., those that require little cooking, such as leeks, onions, and mushrooms. This will not work with turnips, beans, or broccoli —those vegetables would have to be parboiled before sautéing. Of course, there are exceptions to every rule.

Gratin

Gratin is an oven preparation. Mix parboiled vegetables with béchamel sauce, place in a pan, and top with cheese or bread-crumbs or both. Bake in a 400°F (205°C) oven until the top is a nice brown color.

Steamed

Steaming is the easiest preparation, one that lends itself to all vegetables. Steam only to al dente—oversteaming will turn vegetables brown.

Braised

Braising is another oven preparation, but the vegetables are part of a specific dish and are cooked with the meat. Mix raw vegetables with stock or red wine sauce and place in the bottom of a pan. Place meat on top, cover with aluminum foil or lid, and cook.

Glazed

This preparation begins on the stove and finishes in the oven and can be used with all non-starch vegetables. It imparts a sweet flavor. Sauté the vegetables in butter or olive oil, then add sugar and caramelize. Add some wine and stock, transfer to a baking dish, cover with aluminum foil, and place in oven. While cooking, turn the vegetables so that all sides are glazed.

Stuffed

This is another oven preparation in which we stuff the vegetable with a farce of meat, fish, or a different vegetable. When using a meat farce, you may want to precook the farce to avoid over-cooking the vegetables while thoroughly cooking the meat.

Creamed

This preparation is done on the stove and makes vegetable dishes that go well with roasted meats. Cut the vegetable into julienne and sauté in butter. Add some chicken or vegetable stock and cook until the vegetables are al dente. Remove the vegetables and add some milk or cream to the stock. Reduce to desired thickness and season with salt, pepper, and nutmeg. Strain the sauce through a sieve and add to vegetables.

Puree

I think of this as a winter preparation, but it can be of use in the summer as well. Here we use ⅔ vegetable to ⅓ starch such as rice or potatoes. Boil the vegetable together with the starch. Strain then dry in a pan on the stove, being careful not to burn them. Place in a food processor and blend. Finish with a bit of cream and desired seasoning. Reheat in a double boiler.

Parboiled

For this method, we partially cook the vegetables in boiling water, then cool them down in ice water to stop the cooking process. For green vegetables, use a little more water and cook for a shorter period to retain as much color as possible. All vegetables should be cooked al dente. Now sauté in butter or olive oil with a little chopped shallot.

Prepared in Sauce

Here we sauté the vegetable on the stove in a pot and then add the sauce of beef stock or tomato. Reduce the heat and simmer slowly until vegetables are fully cooked. This preparation does not require an al dente outcome—the vegetables will become one with sauce.

Grilled

Here we cook raw vegetables with olive oil on a hot grill. This preparation works well for the same vegetables you would sauté, i.e., those that may also be eaten raw. Slice the vegetables on the thin side and keep the grilling time short so as not to burn your vegetables. If you want to add herbs for flavor, use fresh ones and add them to the olive oil used for grilling.

The best fish is the freshest, and I always take advantage of what an area has to offer. In the Caribbean, we sometimes fish ourselves. When in the Mediterranean, I use the regional fish in the recipes. You can use whatever fresh fish is available, but I recommend the use of strong fish. Not strong in flavor, but strong in structure, fish that won't flake too much during preparation.

I like to grill, panfry, or bake fish and am not too keen on poached or steamed preparations. I also like to use beef or other meat stock in preparation to boost the flavor and character of the fish. Lobster and scallops go well with cream and butter sauces.

seafood

Ragout of Shrimp with Young Vegetables in Light Wine Sauce

½ kilo (about 1 pound) jumbo shrimp
1 spoonful olive oil
2 spoonfuls chopped tarragon
splash of white wine
240 milliliters (about 8 fluid ounces) fish stock
200 grams (about 7 ounces) cream
1 leek
2 tomatoes
100 grams (almost ¼ pound) shiitake mushrooms
1 onion, peeled and diced

Peel the shrimp, remove the heads, and devein. Combine them with the olive oil and half the tarragon. Set aside to marinate.

Sauté the shrimp peels and heads in a pan, adding a splash of white wine. Add fish stock and reduce. Add the cream and cook for about 5 more minutes. Strain.

Clean and julienne the leek. Peel, seed, and dice the tomato. Clean the mushrooms and julienne the tops. Add to salted leek.

Peel the onion. Lightly sauté the onion, then add the marinated shrimp and panfry. In a separate pan, sauté the leek.

Combine the shrimp and leek. Add the cream sauce and tomato. Serve in a deep dish. Garnish with remaining tarragon.

I usually serve this ragout as an interim course in a menu, but it can also be served as a main course with a starch. While some of the ingredients are prepared separately, they all end up in the same pot for finishing.

Grilled Red Snapper with Tropical Tapenade

6 pieces red snapper, 200 grams (almost ½ pound) each

olive oil

3 pinches Chinese five-spice

salt and pepper

2 sweet potatoes

1 leek, julienned

½ mango, peeled, seeded, and cubed

1 pinch nutmeg

¼ pineapple, peeled and diced

1 dollop butter

2 spoonfuls sesame seeds

240 milliliters (about 8 fluid ounces) Sauce Aigre Doux (see page 26)

splash of red cabbage juice (red cabbage cooked in orange juice
    and strained), optional

This is a European-style Caribbean preparation with classic vegetables and fruits. Because I find that fish and fruit are not always the best combination, I make a pungent fish, which will go better with fruit than a mild fish does.

To prepare the snapper for grilling, marinate it in a mixture of olive oil, five-spice, and salt and pepper.

Bake the sweet potatoes until they are easily pierced. Cut into 1 ¼-millimeter (½-inch) slices. Lightly sauté the leek, then add mango, salt, pepper, and nutmeg. In a separate pan, sauté the pineapple in butter and add sesame seeds. Cook until somewhat pasty.

Color the sauce aigre doux with red cabbage juice, if available.

Grill the snapper on one side on a hot grill for about 6 minutes, until you see the grill marks. Remove from grill and bake on a tray at 205°C (400°F) for about 4 minutes.

Serving
Place a little bit of leek in the center of the plate and put the fish on top, grilled side up. Arrange the vegetables above the fish with sweet potato in middle, pineapple on one side, and mango and leek on the other. Drizzle sauce around the plate.

Panfried Sole with Sautéed Pears and Pine Nuts

18 sole fillets (3 per person), about 200 grams (½ pound total)
butter
salt and pepper
2 pears
1 garlic clove, chopped
1 pinch ground clove
1 ladle beef stock
1 spoonful pine nuts
3 potatoes
1 pinch nutmeg
1 bunch green asparagus
1 spoonful chives, chopped fine

Fold each piece of sole into thirds, forming a roll. Panfry the sole in butter with salt and pepper.

Clean the pears, peel, remove the seeds, and slice thinly. Sauté in a little butter with garlic and clove, then add beef stock and pine nuts.

Peel the potatoes and boil whole. Once cooked, mash with salt, pepper, nutmeg, and butter.

Blanche the asparagus, and add butter and chives.

Serving
Place the pear and pine nut composition on the plate and put the fillets, folded edges down, on top. Form the potatoes into small quenelles and place beside fish. Place asparagus beside potatoes.

This is a dish that I included on my restaurant menu card for an exam during my last year at school. A jury of restaurant owners then reviewed the menu cards. In those days, nouvelle cuisine was in its infancy, and this was considered a very modern and advanced dish. The garlic and clove will take some of the sweetness from the fruit, making a stronger preparation.

Oven Baked Sea Bass Marinated in Champagne and Lavender

*6 pieces boneless sea bass, 1,200 grams (about 2 ½ pounds) total,
 cut into triangles*
2 glasses champagne
1 spoonful lavender
2 fennel bulbs
splash of olive oil
1 zucchini
1 tomato
2 ladles fish stock

Marinate the fish in champagne and lavender.

Julienne the fennel and lightly sauté in olive oil.

Clean and slice the zucchini. Peel, seed, and chop the tomato. Combine with zucchini and set aside.

Remove lavender seeds from marinated fish. Place the fennel in a baking pan and put fish on top. Add remaining champagne marinade and fish stock. Cover with aluminum foil and bake at 205°C (400°F) for about 5 minutes. Add the zucchini and tomato mixture and bake for another 5 minutes, until fish is cooked but still tender.

Serving
Place fish on a bed of fennel in deep plates. Garnish with zucchini and tomato mixture and broth. Make sure there is no lavender left in the fish—lavender is very bitter and will ruin the meal.

I made this for a Monaco Yacht Club competition. The criterion was to create a Provençal and Mediterranean dish that incorporated champagne. I thought of the lavender fields of Provence, and this dish was born.

Grilled Scallops with French Vegetable Salsa and Beurre Blanc

12 scallops, cleaned

splash of olive oil

salt and pepper

½ cucumber, chopped

½ avocado, chopped

½ red pepper, chopped

½ green pepper, chopped

1 tomato, peeled and chopped

1 clove garlic, chopped fine

1 handful parsley, chopped fine

½ onion, chopped fine

75 milliliters (about 2 ½ fluid ounces) vinegar

splash of white wine

2 spoonfuls chilled butter

Prepare the scallops for grilling by marinating in olive oil, salt, and pepper.

To make the salsa, combine the cucumber, avocado, red and green peppers, tomato, garlic, and parsley. Chop mixture until it is pulpy. Add a bit of olive oil, salt, and pepper. Cover and refrigerate until ready to serve.

For the beurre blanc, put onion, vinegar, and white wine in small saucepan and reduce to about half. Stir in butter. (Golden rule: Never boil beurre blanc!)

Grill scallops on one side only on hot grill. Serve grilled side up.

Serving
Put salsa in center of plate. Place scallops on the salsa. Drizzle the beurre blanc around the composition.

This can be a starter or a second course in a menu. Served with potatoes or pasta, it becomes a main course. I grill or panfry on one side only to prevent the scallops from drying out. The butter will add moisture, and I find that cream or butter sauce goes well with seafood. Always use fresh scallops. Scallops that have been frozen contain a lot of water. Always rinse fresh scallops under the faucet, then dry them well on paper towels. Panfry or grill them at a very high temperature.

Panfried Tuna with Green Peppercorn Sauce

6 tuna steaks, about 150 – 200
grams (6 – 7 ounces) each

3 Roma tomatoes

6 broccoli spears

butter

salt and pepper

1 pinch nutmeg

2 potatoes

2 spoonfuls parsley, chopped

3 small turnips

1 spoonful sugar

splash of white wine

2 ½ ladles beef stock

1 spoonful green peppercorns

splash of whiskey

splash of cream

Lightly panfry the tuna on both sides to medium rare, being careful not to dry it out.

Cut the tomatoes in half and roast in oven for about 15 minutes.

Blanche broccoli spears and toss with a little butter, salt, pepper, and nutmeg.

Peel the potatoes and boil whole until they can be easily pierced. Cool down and cut into thin slices. Panfry potatoes in olive oil until golden brown. Add half the chopped parsley, plus salt and pepper to taste.

Peel and wash the turnips. Cut in half and lightly sauté in butter. Add sugar and caramelize, then add a splash of white wine. Put the turnips in a baking pan, add ½ ladle beef stock, and cover with aluminum foil. Bake at 205°C (400°F) for about 20 minutes.

For the sauce, place peppercorns and whiskey in small saucepan. Cook to reduce. Add remaining beef stock and reduce until thickened. Add a splash of cream to change the color. Add remaining parsley before serving.

Serving
Put the tuna in the lower middle of plate. Place the vegetables above the tuna with turnips on left, potatoes in center, and broccoli on right side. Drizzle sauce over tuna.

When panfrying tuna, I try to keep it a little rare in the middle; well-done tuna tends to be dry. Tuna is one of my favorite fishes, and it lends itself to many different preparations, such as tartars and sushi. I buy the small tenderloin of tuna, which contains fewer veins and has a nice smooth structure.

*B*ecause I'm preparing food on a boat, I tend to serve more fish and seafood than meat. But I do enjoy preparing fowl, poultry, lamb, and other meats. In fact, I have adapted many traditional meat preparations to my fish and seafood recipes. I tend to use meat preparations more as a main course than any other course in a menu. While quail or other poultry could function as a starter, beef, lamb, fowl, and game are reserved for main courses. Starting a menu with steak au poivre vert would ruin your appetite.

These recipes include vegetable preparations, but there are others to choose from. I prepare vegetables to accompany meat in many different ways, and those methods are outlined on pages 86 – 87.

beef and fowl ✕ 103

Duck Breast with Feta and Dill

2 whole duck breasts
200 grams (7 ounces)
   feta cheese, diced
3 spoonfuls dill, chopped
splash of olive oil
salt and pepper
4 handfuls spinach
1 spoonful butter

1 eggplant
1 pinch nutmeg
2 ladles beef or duck stock
1 potato
6 large cauliflower florets
1 handful sugar
splash of white vinegar
2 spoonfuls Metaxa

I came up with this dish while cruising the Greek Isles. Instead of doing the classic canard a l'orange, I decided to experiment with local products. When trying new dishes, it's important to keep an eye on the combination of colors and flavors. While cheese is a fine complement for meat, it doesn't usually work with fish.

Remove two-thirds of the fat from the duck breasts. Marinate the breasts in feta, dill, olive oil, salt, and pepper for 1 to 2 hours.

Remove stems from spinach and wash in cold water up to three times to make sure all sand is removed. Sauté spinach in a little butter, salt, and pepper. Peel the eggplant and cut into cubes. Sauté it in a little olive oil, salt, pepper, and nutmeg. When slightly brown, add a small amount (½ ladle) of stock and allow to simmer 5 to 7 minutes until soft and pasty—undercooked eggplant is tough to eat.

Peel the potato and boil it whole. When it has cooked enough to be easily pierced, slice it equally, one slice per person.

Boil the cauliflower until it is softened. Cool down a little and use a small ladle to form into individual servings. Brush with salt, pepper, and butter.

Caramelize the sugar. Add vinegar and Metaxa, then the remaining stock. Reduce to a consistency that will coat the back of a wooden spoon.

Finishing
Remove the duck breasts from marinade and panfry them, adding a little stock. Reserve the marinade. When the breasts are seared on both sides, bake them at 205°C (400°F) for 5 to 7 minutes. Reheat the vegetables and sauce. Slice the breasts and arrange them in a fan pattern on a plate. Place vegetables above the meat with potatoes in the center. Add reserved marinade to sauce and dress over duck.

Wrapped Tournedos in Filo with Onion Mushroom Truffle Duxelles

6 tournedos of beef, 150 – 200
grams (about ½ pound) each

1 onion

250 grams (about 9 ounces)
    shiitake or other mushrooms

truffle oil

1 spoonful butter

a little fresh truffle, finely
    chopped (if available)

splash of cream

6 sheets filo dough

1 egg yolk

1 potato

1 zucchini

6 slices pumpkin

3 heads Belgian endive

2 ladles beef stock

1 tomato, peeled, seeded,
    and cubed

chopped parsley for garnish

In this recipe I use
Wellington in individual
portions. Steak is a hearty
meat, very masculine in its
way, and not many different
preparations are possible.
I like steak cooked rare–
when well done it loses a
lot of its character. Steak
goes well with vegetables,
and potatoes are the best
choice for starch.

Panfry the beef on both sides until it is seared. Each piece of
meat will require its own cooking time, so pay close attention.

Peel and dice the onion. Clean and chop the mushrooms. Sauté
the onion and mushrooms in truffle oil and butter. Add a splash
of cream and cook until pastelike. At the end, add a little truffle.

Lay out 6 sheets of filo dough. Place beef in center of dough and
cover with ¾ of the mushroom and onion mixture. Close the
dough around the beef, brush with egg yolk, and bake it on a
tray at 205°C (400°F) until dough is browned.

Boil the potato until it can be easily pierced, then slice.
Cut the zucchini into 6-mm (¼-inch) slices. Peel the pumpkin
and slice it to match the potato and zucchini. Slice the endives
lengthwise. Remove and discard the hearts and bottom.

Brush the vegetables with truffle oil on two sides and grill them
on each side.

To make the sauce, put salpicon (leftover onion and mushroom
mixture) and beef stock in a saucepan and reduce.

Serving
Place some sauce in the center of the plate and put one tournedo
on top. Arrange the vegetables above the meat with the potato
in the center. Garnish with tomato and parsley.

*T*his section is very broad and includes a
lot of different skills—ice cream, fruit preparations, pastry, and chocolate. While most
restaurants have a pastry chef to take care of
desserts, on the yacht I do all that myself. I
consider dessert a very important course—it
is the last dish the guest will see and it has to
leave a good impression. But I'm careful not
to be extreme. The main course remains the
principal part of the meal.

desserts

Banana Crème Caramel with Caramel Ice Cream

5 ripe bananas

½ liter (about 2 ¼ cups) Crème Renversée (see below)

parchment paper

Caramel Ice Cream (see page 127)

200 milliliters (about 1 cup) Créme Anglaise (see page 125)

1 spoonful espresso coffee grounds

Blend bananas with the crème renversée. Scoop into ramekins. Place on a large tray with parchment paper on the bottom. Fill the tray halfway with water. Bake at 93°C (200°F) for about 20 to 30 minutes. To check for readiness, prick with the point of a knife. When nothing sticks to the knife, it's done. Remove from oven and refrigerate on a tray.

To make the coffee sauce, add espresso that has been dissolved in a bit of water to the crème anglaise.

To serve, remove flan from ramekins, add a scoop of ice cream, and coat with sauce.

Crème Renversée

This is a classic flan caramel recipe

4 whole eggs

8 egg yolks

500 grams (3 ¾ cups) sugar

1 liter (about 1 ¼ quarts milk)

Mix the eggs and egg yolks with the sugar.

Bring milk to a boil. Add 2 ladles of boiled milk to the egg mixture and blend will, then add the egg mixture to the rest of the milk.

Pour the mixture out into 12 ramekins. Place the ramekins on a tray with parchment paper at the bottom, then fill the tray a third of the way full with water. Bake at 150°C (300°F) until a knife inserted comes out clean. Remove from oven, place on another tray, and refrigerate until cold and ready to serve.

Here I use a flan caramel recipe with bananas. It is still a classic dessert, and one of the first I learned at school. It is quite light, and the perfect ending to almost any meal.

Figs in Coffee, Cinnamon, and Brandy Sauce

■

10 milliliters (about ⅓ ounce) brandy
1 spoonful sugar
1 spoonful coffee
1 stick cinnamon
18 figs (3 per person)
10 milliliters (about ⅓ ounce) fresh cream
Ginger-Raisin Ice Cream (see page 127)

Put the brandy, sugar, coffee, and cinnamon in a saucepan. Reduce over medium heat. Cut the tops off the figs and add figs and tops to sauce. Cook for a couple of minutes. Do not overcook or they will fall apart. Remove the figs and fig tops. Add cream to sauce and stir.

Place figs on a large, deep plate. Fill each with a small scoop of ice cream. Place the fig tops over the ice cream. Dress with sauce.

DESSERTS

Here is an elegant fruit preparation with ice cream that will add a special touch to dessert. The colors blend well, and it is a simple and light preparation with a lot of flavor.

Soup of Strawberry, Dried Cherry, Banana, and Walnut

For this preparation you may use any kind of fresh fruit, dried fruit, or nut. It can be made in any season, and the butter at the end adds a very special touch.

½ liter (about 2 ¼ cups) orange juice

1 glass white wine

3 spoonfuls sugar

250 grams (about 9 ounces) strawberries

2 bananas

1 handful walnuts

150 grams (about 5 ounces) dried cherries

4 basil leaves, chopped

1 pinch chilled butter

To make the soup, put orange juice, white wine, and sugar in a saucepan. Bring to a boil and reduce.

Clean and slice the strawberries. Slice the bananas.

Chop the walnuts into small chunks. Add strawberries, bananas, walnuts, and dried cherries to boiling soup, remove from heat, and let stand for 5 minutes. Add basil and butter. Scoop into deep ice cream dishes.

Option
Serve ice cream on the side or on top of the fruit and soup.

Mousse Tropicale

■

1 tin sweet coconut paste (found in Chinese grocery stores)

1 tin sweet coconut meat in juice

chopped seeds from 1 vanilla stem

1 layer Plain Génoise (see page 125)

6 leaves or 2 packets gelatin

20 milliliters (about ½ fluid ounce) Malibu liqueur

4 egg whites

1 spoonful sugar

400 milliliters (about 13 fluid ounces) whipping cream

½ of ripe mango, sliced thin lengthwise

Place coconut paste, coconut meat, and vanilla seeds in a large mixing bowl.

Prepare a springform with the layer of génoise at the bottom.

If you're using gelatin leaves, soak for 10 minutes in cold water and then add to Malibu liquor over medium heat. For powder, dissolve the gelatin in the Malibu liquor over medium heat.

Whip the egg whites with sugar until they form peaks. Whip the cream set aside in refrigerator.

Add the gelatin to the coconut in mixing bowl. Fold in half the egg whites, then the whipped cream, and finally the remaining egg whites.

Spread half the mousse over the génoise, layer the mango over the mousse, then cover with remaining mousse. Refrigerate until ready to serve. Serve with ice cream.

This is a very simple but distinctive dessert. The coconut flavor is one of a kind, and the egg whites keep it light.

White Chocolate and Dried Cranberry Tart

1 layer Chocolate Génoise (see page 126)
1 recipe White Chocolate Ganache (see recipe below)
250 grams (about 9 ounces) dried cranberries
100 grams (3 ½ ounces) whipped cream
Honey Ice Cream (see page 127)

Prepare a springform pan and put a layer of chocolate génoise in the bottom.

Prepare the white chocolate ganache as described below. Stir in cranberries, then fold in whipped cream. Pour the ganache over the génoise. Refrigerate until firm. To serve, remove ring, slice, and add honey ice cream on side.

White Chocolate Ganache

250 grams (about 9 ounces) cream
100 grams (¾ cup) sugar
1 milliliter (about 3 ½ fluid ounces) Marsala
250 grams (about 9 ounces) white chocolate
100 grams (3 ½ ounces) butter, melted
juice of 1 lemon

Boil the cream with sugar and Marsala. Remove from stove, add chocolate, and stir until chocolate is melted. Add melted butter and then lemon juice. Let stand for 5 to 10 minutes.

DESSERTS

The white chocolate preparation I create here is smooth, but not like fudge. As with most chocolate concoctions, it is a bit heavy, so make sure you serve small portions. It also helps to serve the dessert very cold—cold creates the impression of lightness. To keep everything together, I start with a layer of génoise.

Terrine of Papaya and Banana with Vanilla

5 *ripe bananas*
2 *small ripe papayas*
1 *glass white wine*
1 *vanilla bean*

Slice the banana in half lengthwise. Peel the papayas, remove the stone, and slice. Put in a bowl and add the wine. Remove the vanilla seeds from the bean and add to the fruit. Toss well so the seeds are equally divided. Place the fruit in a terrine lined with plastic film. When filled, close the film and put in the refrigerator with a second terrine pot filled with water on top. (See instructions for Terrine of Tomato, Mozzarella, and Basil on page 57.) Chill overnight.

To serve, remove from terrine and slice. Place a slice in center of plate and drizzle the plate with some crème anglaise.

Here I use the same process, en presse, that is described for the terrine on page 57. This terrine will work with any soft fruit. Citrus fruits do not work, but if you want to use apples, you can try poaching them first. Sugar and liquor provide additional flavor and juice. You may try substituting cilantro for the basil—both work well in sweet preparations.

Strawberry Pastry with Strawberry Salsa and Vanilla Ice Cream

450 grams (about 1 pound) strawberries (⅔ for pastry, ⅓ for salsa)
200 grams (1 ⅓ cups) sugar
6 egg whites
200 grams (about 7 fluid ounces) whipping cream
6 leaves or 2 packets gelatin
10 milliliters (about ⅓ fluid ounce) strawberry liqueur
2 layers Plain Génoise (see page 125)
vanilla ice cream

Blend ⅔ of the strawberries in a food processor and set aside.

Place a pinch of sugar in a bowl, add the egg whites, and whip until frothy. Be careful not to overbeat. Halfway through the process, add remaining sugar little by little and beat until the whites form soft peaks.

Whip the cream until it forms peaks.

Soak gelatin in cold water for 10 minutes, then dissolve in the liqueur over medium heat. Add to blended strawberries. Mix in half of the egg white mixture, add whipped cream, then add remaining egg white mixture. Prepare a springform pan with a layer of génoise at the bottom. Brush the génoise with some liqueur, then cover with half the fruit composition. Top with the second layer of génoise and fill with remaining fruit composition. Refrigerate overnight.

To make the salsa, chop the remaining strawberries and sprinkle with a spoonful of sugar.

To serve, slice pastry, add a scoop of vanilla ice cream, and top with salsa.

DESSERTS

When making fruit pastry, I use only the whites of eggs because the yolks interfere with the color of the fruit. I choose a liqueur made from the same fruit to enhance the flavor. I also like to reserve a little of the fresh fruit to serve with the finished dessert and ice cream.

Crème Anglaise

8 egg yolks

350 grams (about 2 ⅓ cups) sugar

1 vanilla stem

1 liter (about 1 ¼ quarts) milk

Whip the egg yolks and sugar together.

Bring milk and vanilla to a boil. Add 2 ladles of boiled milk to the yolk mixture and blend well, then add egg mixture to the rest of the milk. This procedure will gradually warm the eggs and prevent them from scrambling. Warm over medium heat and stir with a wooden spoon, paying attention to the bottom of the pot to prevent burning.

To check for readiness, coat a wooden spoon with the mixture. Draw a line horizontally through the back of the spoon with your finger. When the top layer stays on top and doesn't run down to the bottom, the anglaise is ready.

Remove from the stove and transfer into another container to stop boiling process. Remove the vanilla stem, mixing the seeds into the créme.

Plain Génoise

5 whole eggs

200 grams (1 ½ cups) sugar

40 grams (¼ cup) flour

25 grams (⅞ ounce) butter, melted

a few drops of vanilla extract

Beat the eggs and sugar together until the mixture has tripled in volume and the color is light. Fold in the flour with a spatula. Make sure it is well blended and that there are no lumps.

Add the butter and vanilla. Spread into a 10 × 14-inch greased baking pan. Cover with a sheet of aluminum foil.

Bake at 205°C (400°F) for 15 to 20 minutes or until cake has risen and is firm to the touch. Remove from oven and cool on wire rack. After 5 minutes, remove foil sheet.

To store génoise, cut into desired shapes and freeze in plastic wrap.

Crème anglaise is a basic sauce for ice creams and other desserts.

Génoise is a basic light sponge cake made with eggs. It is usually layered with mousse. Often, a dessert will have one layer of génoise at the bottom and one in the middle.

While the main purpose of the génoise is to provide structure for the dessert, I like to give it additional flavor. You can add nuts, dried fruit, or dried spices to the plain génoise recipe. To enhance the flavor, you may also add 15 milliliters (½ fluid ounce) of liqueur to the recipe. Add the liqueur with the melted butter.

Ginger and Cardamom Génoise

1 recipe Plain Génoise (see page 125)

1 spoonful ground ginger

2 pinches cardamom

Follow recipe for plain génoise, adding ginger and cardamom to the flour before mixing it with the eggs.

Pistachio Génoise

1 recipe Plain Génoise (see page 125)

200 grams (7 ounces) pistachio nuts, chopped fine

Follow recipe for plain génoise, adding nuts to the egg mixture before folding in the flour.

Chocolate Génoise

1 recipe Plain Génoise (see page 125)

30 grams (about 1 ounce) cocoa powder

Follow recipe for plain génoise, adding cocoa to the flour before mixing it with the eggs.

Almond Génoise

1 recipe Plain Génoise (see page 125)

200 grams (7 ounces) almonds, chopped fine

Follow recipe for plain génoise, adding nuts to the egg mixture before folding in the flour.

Dried Cranberry Génoise

1 recipe Plain Génoise (see page 125)

200 grams (7 ounces) dried cranberries

Follow recipe for plain génoise, adding berries to the egg mixture before folding in the flour.

Basic Ice Cream

Makes 1 liter (about 1 ¼ quarts)
700 milliliters (about 24 fluid ounces) Crème Anglaise (see page 125)
300 milliliters (about 10 fluid ounces) crème fraîche

Caramel Ice Cream

1 recipe Basic Ice Cream (see above)
200 grams (1 ½ cups) sugar
250 milliliters (about 8 ½ fluid ounces) crème fraîche

Heat sugar in saucepan and caramelize. Once the sugar is nice and dark, add the crème fraîche. Cool down and add to the hot anglaise.

Ginger-Raisin Ice Cream

1 recipe Basic Ice Cream (see above)
250 grams (about 9 ounces) sultana raisins
Bacardi dark rum (enough to cover raisins)
1 spoonful ground ginger

Soak raisins in rum for about 1 hour. Add ginger and then raisins to the hot anglaise.

Honey Ice Cream

Honeys from Greece, New Zealand, France, and Belgium each have their own unique flavor. Use whatever you like best, so long as it is liquid.

1 recipe Basic Ice Cream (see above)
4 spoonfuls liquid honey

Add the honey to the hot anglaise.

Coffee Ice Cream

1 recipe Basic Ice Cream (see above)
5 spoonfuls instant coffee

Add the coffee to the hot anglaise.

DESSERTS

Ice creams accent a dessert, and I think most would be naked without it.

Always add flavoring to the hot anglaise. You can use almost any flavor you like, but be careful not to add too much sugar. If the mixture is too sweet, it is difficult to turn in the ice cream machine. Sweet things don't freeze well and will be less firm than a nonsweet blend. Sour or citrus mixtures may crystallize once frozen.

Index

Ingredients.

1 lbs of shrimp.
500gr silver onion
1/2 leak
2 whole peeled tomatoes.
200gr of mushroom. Morell.
1 tablspoon of chopped tarragon.

1. tablespoon oliv
cream. 200gr
~~1/2~~ 1/2 fish sto
~~200g~~

Shrimps we peel and marinated with olive oil o
1 tablespoon of chopped tarragon. Set asid
while preparing ~~the~~ vegts.

Vegts. Clean leak and slice in ~~the leek jul~~ ju
Peel tomato and remove the stone
and dice in cubes.
clean mushroom and leave as a whole.
silver onion we peel

We saute the onion with the shrimp.
We seperatly saute leak julliene and add to